LEMUR

Meredith Costain

illustrated by Stuart Jackson-Carter

WINDMILL
BOOKS

I am a ring-tailed lemur.

2

I have fluffy gray and cream fur and a long black-and-white striped tail. I live in the spiny forests of Madagascar. I love sunbathing. My uncles use their tails to have stink fights! Let me tell you my story.

I am born at the beginning of the rainy season.
I cling to the fuzzy fur of my mother's belly,
drinking her warm milk.

4

5

I grow a little stronger each day.
I'm now old enough to ride on Mom's back.

After eating, we rest in the shade.
We take turns grooming one another.

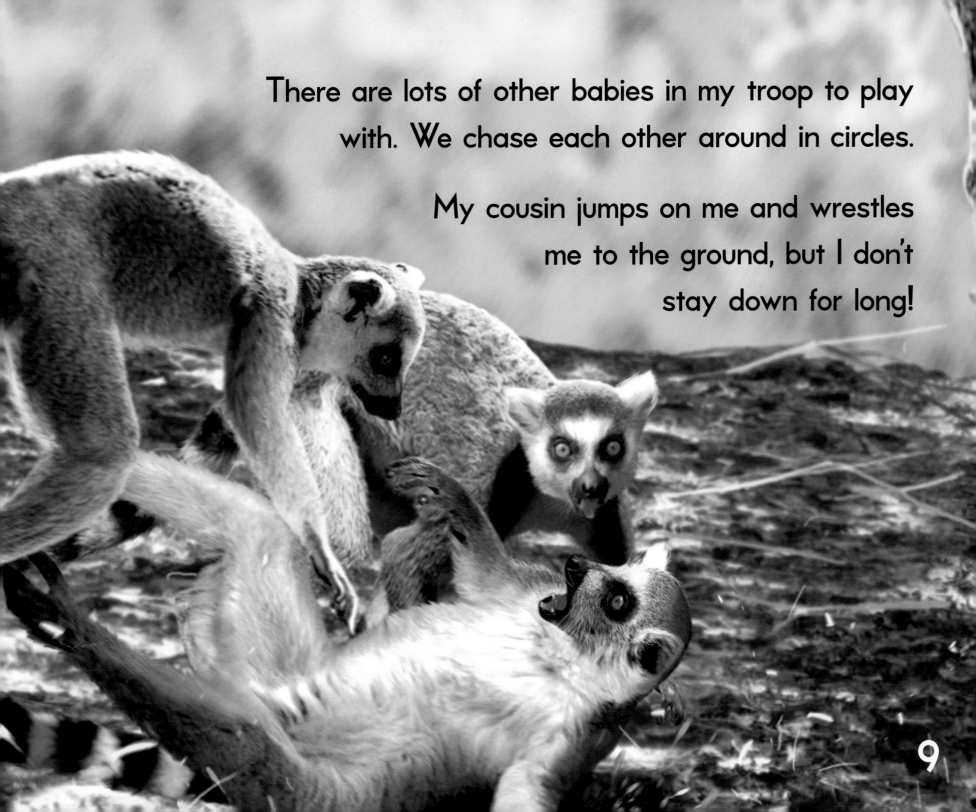

There are lots of other babies in my troop to play with. We chase each other around in circles.

My cousin jumps on me and wrestles me to the ground, but I don't stay down for long!

9

My uncle barks to alert us to danger.
A fossa is on the prowl. My aunties stare
down the intruder until it slinks away.

Each day we travel to a new area of the forest, looking for food. Mom gives me a ride.

We are just settling in when another hungry troop arrives. Mom and I join my aunts in a fierce battle to defend our new range.

15

The next morning, we climb down from our sleeping trees and find a sunny spot on the ground. We're soon warm enough to start our day.

18

After our sunbathing, we search for food.
I like juicy tamarind pods the best.

Three rainy seasons have come and gone. Two of my old playmates leave to join a new troop, on the other side of the spiny forest.

20

21

Two males are fighting for my attention.
They cuff and scratch one another all
day long, then wave their smelly tails
in the air like swords.

22

The stinkiest one wins!

I now have two babies of my own. My sisters and cousins help me to care for them, and I help look after theirs.

24

We have our own big, noisy playgroup!

DID YOU KNOW?

Ring-tailed lemur babies are born in the rainy season.

Mothers are very gentle with their young, grooming them and carrying them on their stomach or back. Babies drink their milk until they are around five months old. Most mothers give birth within a two-week period.

Ring-tailed lemurs are social animals.

They live in groups of from three to 25 animals, called troops. Family members sit close together to groom each other. This forms a bond that holds the group together. Lemurs use their teeth and tongue, rather than their hands, when grooming.

Social play begins around six weeks of age.

Ring-tailed lemurs play-fight from an early age, biting, wrestling, jumping on and chasing one another around in circles. This behavior continues once they become adults. Lemurs are very noisy when they play.

Guards alert the rest of the troop to predators.

Several lemurs stand guard while the rest of the troop is eating. If a predator such as a fossa or hawk approaches, they send out a series of clicks and high-pitched shrieks as a warning signal. The troop will then mob together to scare the predator away.

Ring-tailed lemurs travel around their home range in search of food.

When a large troop travels, they raise their tails in the air like a flag. This helps group members to locate each other if they stray from the path or get left behind. The highest ranking females lead the troop, with low-ranking males at the rear.

Female ring-tailed lemurs dominate the males in their troop.

Females are more aggressive than males, defending their territory against other troops. They leap at and jump-fight the invading females, carrying their babies into battle on their backs rather than leaving them in nests as many other animals do.

27

Ring-tailed lemurs sunbathe in the early morning sunlight.

The forest gets quite cold at night, so ring-tailed lemurs stretch out in the sun each morning to warm up their bodies. To maximize the effect, they sit upright on their haunches with their bellies facing the sun, their arms and legs stretched out to the side.

Ring-tailed lemurs are plant eaters.

They use their hands to gather fruit (especially tamarind pods), flowers, leaves, bark and sap from either the ground or from trees. Occasionally they will eat insects and spiders. They lick rain and morning dew from leaves or drink from a nearby river.

Young males leave their troop once they turn three or four.

Once young males reach maturity, they leave their home troop and join another one. New males will arrive to take their place. Males continue this migration process each mating season. Females, however, stay with their troop their whole life.

Male ring-tailed lemurs hold stink fights in the mating season.

Males cover their long tails with stinky secretions from their wrist glands. They then wave them in the air like smelly swords or flick them at their rivals. The lemur with the stinkiest tail is considered the most powerful and wins mating rights with a female.

Babies are cared for by all the females in a troop.

New mothers allow other females to cuddle and groom their babies in "babysitting" playgroups. This allows them to have a rest and find food, as well as increasing social bonding within the troop.

MEET THE PROSIMIANS!

Ring-tailed lemurs are prosimians, which means "before monkeys." They have features that are more primitive than those of monkeys and apes.

Aye-aye

Lesser bush baby

Golden potto

Red-ruffed lemur

QUIZ

1. Which of these prosimians has black hands, feet, face and tail?

2. Which is the smallest?

3. Which looks the most like a ring-tailed lemur?

4. Which of these prosimians don't have long tails?

Ring-tailed lemur

Scientific name: *Lemur catta*

Skin color: Gray with creamy white bellies and black-and-white ringed tails

Height: 15-18 inches (38-46 cm)

Weight: 5-8 pounds (2.3-3.6 kg)

Size of family group: 3 to 25

Vocal sounds: purr, meow, howl, bark, click, grunt

Habitat: Savanna, deserts, forests, spiny forest, dry scrub, deciduous and gallery forests of southwestern Madagascar

Conservation status: Vulnerable/ Near threatened

Life-span: 50–70 years

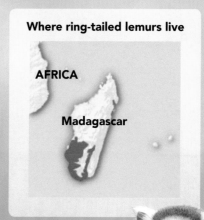

Where ring-tailed lemurs live

AFRICA

Madagascar

Verreaux's sifaka

Slow loris

Philippine tarsier

Ring-tailed lemur

5. Which one has mainly black fur?

6. Which one has large, bat-like ears?

7. Which prosimians have large, staring eyes?

A: 1. Red-ruffed lemur 2. Philippine tarsier 3. Verreaux's sifaka 4. Golden potto, slow loris 5. Aye-aye 6. Lesser bush baby 7. All of them!

31

GLOSSARY

alert	to warn of approaching danger
cuff	slap, strike
fossa	catlike predator from Madagascar
groom	to remove dirt and parasites from the fur
intruder	an unwanted visitor
prowl	to move around stealthily in search of prey
slinks	sneaks around
spiny forest	a dry region of Madagascar with thorny, woody plants
tamarind	fleshy, juicy fruit of the tamarind tree, with a hard, brown shell
troop	group of ring-tailed lemurs

Published in 2017 by **Windmill Books**,
an Imprint of Rosen Publishing
29 East 21st Street, New York, NY 10010

Creative Director Sue Burk
Managing Editor Averil Moffat
Senior Editor Barbara McClenahan
Consultant Dr. George McKay
Design Concept Cooling Brown Ltd
Designer Gabrielle Green
Images Manager Trucie Henderson
Illustrations Stuart Jackson Carter
    except Meet the Prosimians Family pages.

Cataloging-in-Publication Data
Names: Costain, Meredith. | Jackson-Carter,
  Stuart, illustrator.
Title: Lemur / Meredith Costain; illustrated by
  Stuart Jackson-Carter.
Description: New York : Windmill Books, 2017. |
  Series: Wild world
Identifiers: ISBN 9781499482157 (pbk.) |
  ISBN 9781499482164 (library bound) |
  ISBN 9781508193043 (6 pack)
Subjects: LCSH: Lemurs--Juvenile literature.
Classification: LCC QL737.P95 C69 2017 | DDC
  599.8'3--d23

Manufactured in the United States of America

CPSIA Compliance Information: Batch #BW17PK: For Further Information contact Rosen Publishing, New York, New York at 1-800-237-9932